the red flower

...

the red flower

lili marie

Copyright © 2018 by Lili Marie

All rights reserved.

This book may not be reproduced or used in any manner whatsoever without the express written permission of the author except for quotes and/or reviews.

First Printing: 2018

ISBN: 978-1-797-96804-9

instagram: twistedlilac
email: x3oheartx@gmail.com

many moons ago
once upon a moment
in another life

...these are the ways i loved.
and didn't.

twisted lilac

for her,
Love didn't have to be
forever always.

because the moon
is an eternal soulmate
and somehow that's enough.

she just wanted
to meet someone
that tore off a piece
of her existence.

and made her think
that she has loved
the wrong color
all of her life.

sapphire dots

it may have just been
a simple smile.

but it was the divine spell
that led me into
a soft dark tumbling
into a tranquil warmth.

oh, those darling dimples
must hold fascinating stories.

but all i want to do
is dive into the left one
and float
within the waves

of a Spanish dream.

empty skin

lately,
too many words have been

dripping
falling
dangling

but never soaking
into each other.
and it makes me miss the days
your fingertips
rolled down my spine
as you secretly blew
loved-filled wishes
that got caught
in the curls of my hair.

but i guess our scars
never learned how to be
a safe place for the other.

slice of red

because
every thought of you
is shaped like a gray blade.
so, walk past my cage

one
more
time

and let me show you
the ways i believe
that happiness is a bleeding change.

iridescent high

i did not want
you or us,
but when you smiled,

the entire earth
moved
beneath my skin.

and i hoped that you heard it
within your thoughts
when i said,
"unzip
this porcelain skin
this straight jacket
this hiding place

and dance unholy
forever
with my soul."

galactic vibe

she whispers
"make music for me".

he turns off the world
and turns up the Love.
they peel away their worries
and their souls dance
on ripples of moonlight.

pieces of bright
speckle her sighs
as they move
to the melodies

of a diamond moon.

lil twisted thoughts

there are times when i want to wrap the sun around him and squeeze tight. i want to summon every hellfire heart'ed woman to scream at him with their eyes. i want to ask the ocean to dive into him and blot out his soul. i want to stuff that beautiful mouth with the prettiest wildflowers til his face turns cobalt blue. twist his veins. pinch his voice. string him high like the spells on Halloween night. but then there are those times that he is a charming dark and calm. when he looks at me, with Spanish eyes, i fall in love again. when he touches me, i soften in the most delicious ways. the moonbeams dance around him reminding me that i have found my home.

sacred melody

a
seashell
grenade

is three words

to
describe
their
Love.

twilight sun

separated by miles,
and i think of him and smile.

he is such a delectable dark.
i want to walk the roads of his skin,
where the moon shines

with an eerie grin.

to feel his touch
soft, seductive
like the accent

of the night's whisper.

blue coffee

such a brilliant color

of strangeness,
when he talks about
symbols and definitions

opposite of mine.

and i secretly
can't stop listening.

hey boy, come a little closer.
saturate my existence
with your dreams and fantasies.

drip drop into me
over and over again.

the wonderland game

of course
he paid no attention to the

"dangerous! broken!" sign
that my eyes wore.

and walked up my being,
jumping in & out
of my ribs
hopping across scars
until we were eye to eye.

then he dared me
to meet him

in the darkest corner of Love.

passion bubbles

he tells me that he wants
to get lost in my hair.

i grin, telling him
"it's a crazy world in there,
the butterflies bite."
he rolls his eyes smiling.
i roll mine.

then he playfully starts to chase me
and we are running
faster than a speed limit sign,
laughing like maniacs
into a field of tall grass and wildflowers.

then i stopped, when i saw him
jump over the purple ones
leaving them to dance in our wind.
and leaving me breathless.

lavender heartbeat

between sleeping and waking
it's there.
between the stars and the moon
it's there.
between every single thing
it's there.

you are the why
in all ways.

you are what is spelled
always and again.
you are the smear of silver
across the gods foreheads.

you are the calm
the wild
that breathes inside my words.

amber dreams

and i know
soon,
i will have to shake
the touch of your fingertips
out of my hair.

but not tonight.

let's just lick
the honey-flavored disaster
off of each other's skin.

fairy tale

he is

every shade of sapphire.
a breathless sky.
that pure moment in November.

the outline of my soul.

twisted love

our "i miss you" ways
in shades of stubborn red.

he lets his mouth dive in Tequila
while i drip drop away
acting like this silent distance
means nothing.

together, but alone,
we are tongue-tied at night.

always dying for this thing called Love.

and every morning
finding the sheer beauty
in forgetting to walk away.

midnight joy

we are rolled into one tonight.

and as he holds me,
he says
"this is how the sunlight feels
when it sinks
into a thick beautiful snow."

and my blood sighs.

tequila voo-doo

because
there is no end to the story
that we have started.

and sometimes no dang sense.

if only i could drink
a bottle of Patron,
or two or 3,
until i am sick of Love
inside my skull.

and throwing it all up
also meant,
throwing my feelings for you

out of me.

soul star

madness comes in
all kinds of flavors
and irresistible flaws.

it's hard to not want
to try all of them.

but when you touch me,
i feel myself melting
into a raw power
like silver lightning.

and in your eyes,
i see something higher

than the midnight sky.

strawberry sins

daydreaming
about the reality of you and me.

your kiss tasted just as i imagined

full of terror
moonlit sky
and magic.

with eyes the color
of freshly clawed earth,
making the red in me grin.
our intensity is
savage, satisfying and sweet.

all these thoughts rolling around my mind,
i wonder if my coworker can hear them?

number six

that day in August
was a beautiful heart puff,
full of joyful emotions.
i watched
the beginning of a love story
walk towards me.

the sky sizzled with delight.
the stars twirled in my veins.
and i wrote my name on his palm,
to show him his ending.

he kissed my forehead
making the clouds blush and disappear.
smiling, he got into his Jeep.

and i didn't know how
i was going to exist
until he smiled at me like that

again.

spanish silk

he wore my favorite:
just his voice ... at night.

purple taffy

let's bring the silence
out of the corner

for tonight.

just hush and walk towards me
s l o w,
with eyes hanging onto mine.
wrap yourself around me tight,
the way raindrops
cling to a spiderweb.

the ache for tousled flesh
vibrates in my fingernails.

come here and
shape me into the scent

of "well loved".

moon blossom

this love
for you

distorts me.

i'm breaking into colors
of a happy frenzy.
my darkness is quiet'ing.

and i'm becoming addicted
to the beautiful white stings.

still laying in the grip of night,
but being held

by you.

the rabbit hole

oh little flower of joy
opening inside of me.

my bones are turning into water.
my heart is becoming rich, brown earth.

the images of Love's possibilities
are flowing through me.

and i just want to know,
what the heck are you doing to me?

one red vein

silver blue
deja vu
of our wild and perfect
blending.

when he slid his finger
down my spine,
i instantly felt the threads
inside my bones
wanting to pull him in
to intertwine,

and tie tight.

hi you

somehow
i have crashed into myself.
but i can't tell who felt it first,

you or me.

so whenever you look in the mirror
and see an approaching storm,
the beads of water
throwing themselves
against your reflection.

it's only me just missing you.

pieces of peace

it was almost like, when he appeared,
the words just disappeared.

his existence replaces the meanings of

letters
colors
numbers.

and the first time that we kissed,
on that full moon night,
even the wind seemed to gather itself

to stop and watch
in awe.

invisible ink

tonight,
i don't want to talk.

so i think i'll get my favorite book
and empty it into my Tequila,
to drink and feel
the dizzy sizzle
of words
as they slide down
into forgotten memories

of once upon a time stories.

twang heart

just so you know,

you can never have
too much
Southern Love

inside
your
pen.

you complete me(ss)

another week of torn lilac petals,
and rainbows that hang upside down.

but this world of ours
is folded between passion
and crimson,
a raw that you can taste.

the scars we create
are scented in a golden honey glaze,
so we don't mind the burns.

but right now,
i am wondering
if you are
shattering
in the same amount of pieces

that i am.

crimson curl

a kaleidoscope of tranquil warmth
explodes beneath my skin.

he speaks to me
as if red roses have kissed
the curves of his mouth.

his kiss, the touch of sunset.

those words from his lips
filled
with colors of a flame'ing rainbow.

and i fall into a pretty pile
of blush and heat.

roof top clinks

you.
me.

and a bottle of night
in the middle

of Love's
plush crunch.

no red light

with you,

the wildflowers are scented
in every swirling shade of joy.
the moon shimmers long,
as if dangling by a galactic thread.
the oceans slows and soothes
like a favorite lullaby.
and this magical love-ship
makes me wonder
if you will always heighten
the heartbeats inside me.

oh darling,
while i do love this path we are on,
there are times i want to pause
to grab a handful of white gravel
and throw it at you.
and i'm gona,

so ya better run beautiful boy.

scent of safe

laying on top of his chest,
the walls are quiet.

our breaths dissolve into the night.
and then i hear raindrops fall,
while the beating of his heart

protects
the windows of my soul.

luna gemz

pale cashmere flesh,
swaying beneath a field
of black sparkle.

the stars so bright
they could cut.

and his rhythm sinks into me.
with his eyes, he tells me
he can't get enough of the ways
my body spells Love.
and he's getting envious
of how the dark air
clings to my skin.

my heart smiles
and i grab his hand,
"c'mon baby"
i say,

"teach me something new tonight."

soft onyx

the ways
your voice

and the moon
speak to me

in the same language.

scorpio season

Him.

he has the type of voice
that makes you think of
a moonless black sky,
and the ancient mystery of it.

the stars stand in line
waiting
to jump off the edge of night.

and hoping to fall
into the sweet rush of Wonderland
that is his soul.

white water

he wants a reason
and all i can say is,

it's like the way moonlight
falls through the trees.

you bend into me
and undo me.

i love you
beyond all insanity
and eternity
and reason.

scarlet bouquet

your presence
burns into me

every
single
time.

my comfort,
in the color red.

alcohol lines

his
touch
is
a
1930's
romantic.

the
possibilities
of
Love,

on
a
black
and
white
night.

porcelain shot glass

this feeling
is more than possibility.
it's intense like an immaculate white beast.

it is more gorgeous
than the wings of thunder.
but with blood dripping from its mouth.

my mind is suddenly
the color of whiskey.
and i am love-drunk
inside the bottle of my skull.

but you will never know
because the kiss of your fingers
just told me

that silence can be sexy too.

sweet silver

i feel you,
like a swarm of ghosts
with the sound of gray diamond.

your voice,
the color of lightning
spiraling across the walls of me.

i lay still
to let your darkness devour me.

bind me with your imagination,
your wishes,
your heartbeats

and take us away.

infinite ever

in everything
that i

write
say
feel

pay
attention
to the

i's and u's.

angel flame

the way his touch
can create

a halo
of heat

around the wind.

Lili Marie

i watch him,
the one with
stormy night colored eyes.

the moon asks
"who would want
to be struck
by his lightning?"
i giggle.

ME.

kitten quartz

pale body
in his crisp, white
long-sleeved shirt
with glitter spray in my hair.

c'mere you.
knock at my door.

i'll open up, and be your luna love.

and let you slip the night
right off of me.

cloud eight

and right now,
i am as high
as the sapphire twist
in the sky.

so pull up some space beside me
dearest ghost.
let's have tea time
and talk about
all the colors of lightning.

and why the wildflowers
tell me his name
when i bend down
to ask them theirs.

red roses

you

have
contaminated
me

in
all ways

of tender.

secret petals

short but intense stories
are the best.

little poems too.

or the ones
that you leave tucked
inside the small curve

of my back.

drops of ocean

it saddens me
that i won't
get to kiss you
as many times
as there are
pebbles
of
sand.

rainbow fireflies

impossible you,

like being able to bite
into water.

when did you become so addictive?
why do i crave the Love

found within a merry-go-round night?

zen flower

his smile
is a favorite calm.

spirit lingo

talking to him
was like driving
at night.

there was no true destination,

just the familiarity
of intimacy.

champagne fizz

butterflies
on rainy days,

when he
stares at me

like this.

vanilla fear

imagine
if
emotions
were
attached
to
scent.

china dahlia

my heart,
like a porcelain star
laying
in the palm of your hand.

never close up on me
darling.

i need to breathe in your world.

heart lyrics

after i read a book,
i am changed somehow.
just like when i talk with you.

and i love that.

midnight chandelier

press your palm
against my throat,

to feel the beat
of swirling stars.

and how they wish
to shine in your night

inside a pulse of eternal love.

humble shamrocks

one kiss
was all it took.
only one.

it was full,
complete
and haunting

just like la Luna.

butterfly bottles

he speaks.

and the whole world
drops into dust.
people pop like bubbles.

he is all that i see.
he is all that i hear.

my flesh
turns into a river
of a hundred blushing petals
when his voice
finds its way

into the curve of my neck.

velvet second

like dewdrops
that find each other
on violet petals,

you and i

will remain a wish
at midnight hour,
pressed
between forever

and always.

sterling symbol

i promise that every night
i will hush and close my eyes,
laying still.

so you can put your hand
on my chest
to feel the pulse in my heart.

this delicate jerk
of how the center in me

will always submit to you.

two eternities

he tasted of
vanishing memories

anger
hope

and home.

lit light

the sky burns
with the scent of Tequila.

the stars shine
like a thousand shot glasses.

and i want to know,
what is it
that you truly wish for?

snowflake sun

give me a reason

to melt
into your tomoro
like a Winter horizon.

because
my reasons
for agree'ing
to all the parts
of this

are starting
to disappear.

capricorn ice

a touch
of this man's
fingertips,

and my body
floods
with little shimmering hells.

he makes the lilac in me
drop
into a wild wide red,

making me ache for winter.

no signal

lost
in
the
parking
lot
of
Love.

vegas colors

the blur of white hot dots
that you see
after a toss of the dice.

it was like that.
it was his aura
that made me want to risk it,
to gamble what was left
of my belief about Love.

when he smiled,
he lit up the darkest night in soft red.
he could be my hiding place,
if i needed one.

and he could also be
my heart-brick road to Love.

pink knots

maybe if i write
our names side by side

on white paper
and draw a red circle
around them
on a full moon night
and then shred it
into the amount of days
that we have been apart,

m a y b e

you will find your way back to me.

stop sign

he
is
swimming
against
the
current
of my blood.

wine and crackers

when he sat beside me,
i felt the shift in my breath.
i heard a door open in my soul.
i smelled "a sign" in the air.

and i knew.

the next moment
and my life after that
would never be the same.

the wings of eternity were finally here.
because i have shed myself
in so many ways
a hundred times and again.

and he still hasn't let go of his hold.

table for two

strawberry tea,
a game of Scrabble
and the air
scented

with laughter and love.

the fireflies
light the night
with their smitten faces.

this is us.

temper tantrums

the sound

of
his

"hello"

under
shattered glass.

quiet eyes

when
the fire in me
refuses
to soothe you...

what will happen then?

stoned solo

the ocean
looks different

when our
fingers

aren't laced together.

el tiempo

this red velvet need,
like an ache in flames,
emotions inflamed.

i want to have my flesh

stirred
loved
plucked

by you
like a Spanish guitar

flickering
beneath a moonlit sky.

a new notebook

she's wondering
if she is finally over him

because
today

her tears
refuse

to be swallowed.

room service

the way
thoughts of you
flow
inside of me,

a mixture
of sea and sky.

i want to count
the waves
with you,

to show you
the hidden stories
in numbers.

as we swim
in each other's skin,
under an island moon.

holy art

hearing him laugh
sends my bones
into the softest swirls.

his voice in southern Spanish
is a bouquet of red wine.

and that touch is euphoric,
a cotton candy insanity,
a glorious delicious.

he makes me feel
as if i am
throwing back shots

with every god in the world.

almond twirl

on that night
in room #86,

our eyes met.
our bodies felt.

the earth shifted.
the sky quivered.
the walls caved in.

and there we were,
warm flesh
rolling around
in peeled paint.

when i felt your breath
love on my skin,
it reminded me
of the cherry trees
Neruda once spoke about.

panther moon

my fingers

may be
beautifully
entwined
with his

but

i am
collared
by midnight.

stiletto shot

on a crystal black night,
the stars
spelled out his name.

so she took
her grand-daddy's old rifle
and shot them

one by one.

she gave herself
a gift,
the sound

of peace.

fairy tale blood

you. me. we. us.
a "new love"
and all of its
glorious possibilities.
your smile is the
firefly in my mind.
flickering. tempting. wanting.
i grin at the twirling feelings.
and let the thoughts linger
and wrap around me,
taking me to the soft parts
of Wonderland.
i can see us living
in the abundance of infinity.
but it's not you,
my dazzling "what if",
it's me.
and i have to pull off
these veins of thoughts
one by one
like the petals of a rose.

the green jacket

it
was
because
his type of
c r a z y
felt too good
to completely forget.

black marble

awed by his gift,

giving me
the responsibility
to hold his heart.

sun ray thrill

i've been in love before.

but it was a tiny
heat of pink,
never crimson.

until him.

he made me feel
the lava inside red.

eternal ribbon

i don't know if you knew.

but the first time
you kissed me,
i dissolved.

i was a pale puddle
at the edge of your lips,
waiting for you
to breathe me in.

i had one vision,
to crawl down
your throat
until i reached
the center of you
so we could

exhale together.

road trip

stirring the air,
with my finger
as i think of you.

and the planets
have gotten caught
in my hair

again.

sober shadow

i walked in, saw you smile
and it changed me.
the voices in my head
s c r e a m e d,
trying to find a way out.
and i hated you for months
after that because i never even asked
but was given the answer
"you".
you were meant to exist
with me, in me.
and yes i did try to run away
even tho everything after that moment
turned sapphire, turned into you.
so turn around again,
and say hello to me.
let me see that smile
one more time
and then
forever after that.

the amor

my favorite alcohol
is Tequila.
it is fast, thrilling moments
of a sweet little hellfire
going straight down.
altho, i could put
a straw in the sky
to sip on every
puff of cloud
letting the velvet white
drain into me.
and i can get swirly
off of certain 3am scents
allowing myself to feel cosmic
and try to lick the zen from the air.
but my favorite high
is when he kisses me
after
he has drank his favorite alcohol
Tequila.

charmed poison

that one there
was born

to
hustle
words

without ever
needing
to
say
one.

wildflower brew

the silence between us
shimmers,

an iridescent breath
of the moon.
only we know how
to make the quiet

mysterious
enticing
svelte

because of the
s p e l l
we have over each other.

shattered air

and just like that,
in the snap of lightning,
it was over.
DONE.
we were no longer.
the future was now the dead.
our love and its pieces
floated down
the neighborhood street
and a cat dipped her paw.

cloud puff

you may be
the wrong kind of paradise.

but c'mere boy,
and show me where the lake is.
so we can

inhale
share Love
laugh bright
exhale

and dwindle beside it
beneath
a fading blue sky.

i dare you

stop
staring
at
the
silence.
climb over it
and
stare
at
me.

graffiti hands

all the ways we
d e s t r o y
Love.

and yet are unable
to pull the wreck
out of ourselves.
dig a lot deeper baby.
crawl inside me.
find the places
where there is no mess,
and love me hard

until there is.

listen 101

silly ol him,
oblivious
to how my heart roars

"we are magic"
"we are amazing"
"we are always".

and how it loves him
with diamond confetti tones.

steel paws

so many Texas storms
you watched
from your bedroom window.

and yet
i bet
you still never expected
the one

with a temper
with a love

like Bonnie & Clyde.

italian cream cake

when you hear their voice,
and get the
deep cozy feeling
of being soothed.

he has
the type of eyes
that say
"come outside
to watch the stars
with me."

this man is like
reading Rilke
during a Summer night rain.

and he chose
to be by my side
every night
to read to me.

full moon

the scent
of the night
i met him
is rooted
inside
of my blood.

caramel chalice

when they ask me,
"so why him?"

i say
because
flames are his
power and pleasure.

and
his love
is like
white lightning.

darling mistress

sit quietly with me
for a while
and let's
just count the raindrops
before we go back
to arguing
whose silence started first.

friday promise

when you are near,
the colors of busy
f a d e.
and i just want to be
l o c k e d
inside our "us"
b e h i n d
a black and white door.

the haunted villa

the wonders
from that first kiss.

he tasted
like mystery,
the kind I like
with ghosts and gemstones.
and torn pages
scattered on the floor.

he tasted
like a strawberry night.

he tasted like tomoro.

pinky swear

because
the walls in me paused,

maybe even screamed a little.

but i wasn't afraid or angry
because the air filled
with such a beautiful warmth.
and that's how i knew

it was you, you, you.

cherry mud

so many tiny deaths
occurred in me
along the way,
on the journey to you.

i have finally found
sanctuary
within the dip
of your chest.

my being is now filled,
now cradled
with rich earth
from the raw protection
of your eyes.

cinnamon delight

the ways my stubbornness
is feisty and solid,
like a glass sea

but shatters

into alabaster waves,
softening into
serene ripples

when he kisses my fingers.

water lilies

as it rains,
i'm trying to taste it,

to remind myself
of the time our bodies

were high on alive
and wet like paint.

when your palms
were around my face,

the feeling of adored.

night bright

i hold us, darling
while we are apart.

the moon
glows
with crashing heartbeats.
the night cries stars.
and i catch them,
putting them into
my purple glass jar.

these moments of us
together
through distance

still shine.

red mirror

so here is the thing.
when i left,
i didn't know that the warmth
was going to stay with you.
as a Capricorn, all i know is winter
but i was wildly aware
that it was now cold.
and i hated that i missed
the sun
in your eyes, in your smile.
and the little fires
that lived on the ends
of your fingertips.

i felt a new craving.

i
needed
to
burn.

the last chance

let's
just
hold
each
other
tight
until
we
are

a crumpled breath.

dark forest

the tender way
you whisper curses
with your fingertips
against my flesh.
and i succumb,
cascading

into your palm of night.

luna vida

the night we met,
i was looking for a way out
of my existence
if only for a couple of hours,
under the full moon.
whether you knew
what you were doing, you did it well.
because the answer
to my way out, was to let you in.
you have brought me
symbols
shadows
and dancing fire.
the white rabbit clouds are constant.
and i've seen the moon
fold itself into origami
and dazzle like a holy diamond.
the shades of Love you give
are endless.

skull azucar

candy flavored
voo-doo.

the way his kiss
spins
around
my existence
with the sweetest webs

and no intent
to release me.

good morning

i
love
the
ocean's
moods
and
i
love
you.

dream shells

Spanish vases,
midnight
and other types
of mystical
found
beneath his skin.

summer confession

he looks at me
as if he's discovered my secret.
he stares at me
as if he's found his paradise.

he has a touch that teases
like soft candlelight.
and a mind drenched
with night sky.

and
now
i
know
that Love
was meant
to destroy
oh so beautifully.

party for dos

#ourrelationshipstatus

juggling our machetes
beneath a gray diamond sky.
hips swaying
to the crackle of our grins.
eyes locked and loaded.
and i suddenly wish,
that i was able to stone you
with raindrops.
because that's what we do.
we are insane to each other,
loving the other
beyond the strength of crazy.
existing
on the symbol of infinity.

blue garden

your hands
may hold

haunting memories
past regrets
and future questions

but
it's still the place
i want to sleep in at night.

wake up

bits
of silky white
diamonds
fell
from the sky.

waves of black
s p r e a d
across like wide ribbon.

we thought
it would be like this
forever.

until the moon appeared
and
we were forced
to
face
our
fears.

le pause

the way
he moves
his thumb
a c r o s s
my mouth
and

it all goes silent.

love spots

this man,

sedation
and
enchantment,

devouring my senses
until my soul
is a quivering puddle

with the scent
of his name.

dazzling whirls

and
here you come along
like this tornado
wild, but serene

blowing away my uncertainties
leaving me nowhere to stand

but in your arms.

blush and smirk

he calls me baby.

and my skin
ripples
like river water.

even the piranha
hide their teeth.

bubble bath

darling,

if a day comes
that i am unable
to make the frustrations
go away

then
i will just
sit here with you
and

love you quietly.

the red scarf

my wolf calls me
his luna preciosa.

but i also howl for him.
the center of me aches

for his love
for his touch
for his everything

reaching out
like a feisty 3am.

meant to be

the glass ball
hangs
by a shimmer
in the center
of a crackling dark wide.
and darling
you are chipped

in all the right places.

iceberg pose

when
the
words
cross a boundary
and
everything in you
only
knows
silence
now.

see me

sometimes my soul gets tired.
but when it gets so very tired is when i wish i could quietly slip into the bottom of the prettiest tea cup. no fear of being found by you, of course, because you only drink out of beer bottles and coffee mugs.

darkling dance

we were
nothing but
myth and magic

in a jar of wind.

and you still
couldn't find
the power and faith

in us.

moonbeam wish

dearest Luna,

send me the partner
who desires
to endure,

even when the red
isn't so bright.

glass chimes

not even the stars
that hang
in the Southern sky
contain
as much white gold

as is in his laughter.

glitter rain

when we met
our spirits fused.

it was a type of art,
a divine white horror.

it was the light
of a hundred
flower petals.

a magic
only we
could
create

and
define.

purple wolf

his voice. that voice.
the perfect shade of black.
the howling
you can't escape from.
and never ever want to.

three mouthfuls

c'mere darling
i want to love on you.

let me sip long
and feverishly.

until you are
trickling
out of the corners

of my life.

yellow orbs

their love
is on its death bed.

forgotten
and uncared for.

just like
the tossed rosary beads
the black cats play with
behind the glorious church.

orchid hymn

you and me.

nothing but flowers on fire.
blood spilled at midnight.

the rainbow
inside oil and water.

a l w a y s
taking the others
breath away

because of some
beautiful crazy that we did

again.

pink suede

homesick
for
the
palms
of
his
hands.

the red flower

somehow
Love
entered

my imagination
my veins
my dreams

despite
it never
being given
an invitation.

teacup swirl

this heart
is a mess
of crimson roses

and
fierce wind.

come near.

you look the type
to throw your arms
up

and breathe me in.

white wine

summer nights.
moonlight rinses the earth.

i will help you shine.

just get on the knees of Love
and crawl nearer.

lace and love

tonight
i lay tangled in the floral
of beauty, eagerness, love
and you...
the light i wish to wrap it all in.

submitting to the truth.
surrendering to the reality.
i have fallen in every way
imagine and created for you.

tonight
i am burrowing my spine
into your grasp,
a precious and intricate gift.

Love has made my life need this,
making me want to stay this way.

until the white in the moon falls out.

alpha-bits

do you see them?

the black and white words
tumbling from my lips,
laced in your red iridescent.

these expressions, these emotions
that once hung snug
from the ceiling of my mind,
now loosened
by the dark in your voice.

or was it the stuff called Love?
but
do you see what you've done?

do you see them?

thirty one miles

the bedroom air
is cooler
when you're not here.

the walls whisper
that they miss
the surge
of our sweet savage.

and i miss
laying beside you.

indigo mosaic

my plan
is to know about

the stories
the sorrows
the sunsets

that have stained
your eyelashes.

king godly

ghosts
may drift
into my thoughts.

but only one
entity haunts.

only one
possesses
the castle

of my soul.

sunday night

this Love with you feels holy.

like moonlight
spread across my flesh.

our flame may turn to smoke
but you will always
remain eternal inside of me.

we
will forever be

the scent
of 119 white candles.

...

thank you for reading,
for friendships and for your support.
much love and smiles.

keep writing.

xo,
Lili Marie

ps. i learned. :)

Made in the USA
Middletown, DE
02 March 2019